SCORCHING SUPERCARS

by Steve Goldsworthy

Consultant:
Paul Wallace
Director
Supercar Scene Limited
Winchester, Hampshire, England

CAPSTONE PRESS
a capstone imprint

Edge Books are published by Capstone Press,
1710 Roe Crest Drive, North Mankato, Minnesota 56003
www.capstonepub.com

Library of Congress Cataloging-in-Publication Data
Goldsworthy, Steve, author.
Scorching supercars / by Steve Goldsworthy.
pages cm.—(Edge books. Dream cars)
Summary: "Discusses supercars, including what defines a supercar, models that made
their mark on the supercar world, and how manufacturers continue to bring speed
and performance to the next level for these exclusive sports cars"—Provided by
publisher.
Audience: Ages 8-14.
Audience: Grades 4 to 6.
Includes bibliographical references and index.
ISBN 978-1-4914-2014-0 (library binding)
ISBN 978-1-4914-2185-7 (eBook pdf)
1. Sports cars—Juvenile literature. I. Title.
TL236.G64 2015
629.222'1—dc23   2014021762

Editorial Credits
Carrie Braulick Sheely, editor; Heidi Thompson, designer; Pamela J. Mitsakos, media
researcher; Katy LaVigne, production specialist

Photo Credits
Alamy:© Phil Talbot, 16-17; Corbis: © Transtock/© Wes Allison, 9, Demotix/
© Belinda Hastie, 27, Transtock/© John Lamm,10–11, 19, arabianEye/© Katarina
Premfors, 7 ,© Transtock, 5; Dreamstime:© Chris Nolan, 12, 14; Getty Images: Getty
Images News/Patrick Aventurier, 22–23; Newscom: SIPA/JOFFET EMMANUEL, 13,
EPA/SALVATORE DI NOLF, 21, imago stock&people, 6 , 29, ZUMAPRESS/Denis
Sollier, 24, Splash News/SWNS, 25; Superstock: Transtock, cover

Design Element: Master3D, iconizer (throughout)

Printed in the United States of America in Stevens Point, Wisconsin.
102014   008479WZS15

Table of Contents

WHAT'S SO SUPER ABOUT SUPERCARS?

You sit in the driver's cockpit gripping the leather-wrapped steering wheel. It almost seems like you're in a fighter jet with all the instruments and gauges around you. The monstrous V-12 engine snarls from behind as you press down on the gas pedal. In seconds you're rocketing around a test track at more than 150 miles (240 kilometers) per hour. You're in control of a car that is so far from ordinary that it has a special name—a supercar.

What is a supercar? There isn't one agreed-upon answer. However, supercars usually share a few features. They are rare, high-performance *sports cars*. They come with steep price tags. With flashy features such as wide rear *spoilers* and *gull-wing doors*, supercars are designed for excitement. Most importantly, they are designed for speed. Modern supercars can reach at least 200 miles (322 km) per hour.

Supercars have more in common with race cars than they do with average sports cars. Yet they are built for the streets, not the racetracks. For those wealthy enough to afford them, supercars provide the ultimate driving thrill.

Although many car manufacturers produce supercars, a few companies stand out from the crowd. Ferrari, Lamborghini, Bugatti, and McLaren are legendary names in the supercar market.

Fact >>>>>

Most supercars cost between $350,000 and $5 million.

The Lamborghini Murciélago LP640 has scissor, or "Lambo," doors. These doors lift up vertically.

sports car—a street-legal car that is designed for high performance; most sports cars are small, lightweight, and sleek

spoiler—a wing-shaped part attached to the front or rear of a sports car that improves the car's handling and keeps air from lifting the car off the road

gull-wing doors—car doors hinged at the roof that look like spread bird wings when opened

Unique Cars

Every supercar is unique in design. A supercar can have one of several body styles. Most supercars have mid-engines that are mounted just behind the driver. Other supercars have engines placed farther back or in the front. Most supercars have only two front seats. Others have a single driver's seat and two back passenger seats. Despite all these design options, all supercars are built for speed.

Supercar Name	Number Produced
Lamborghini Veneno	3
SSC Ultimate Aero	24
McLaren F1 LM	5
Maybach Exelero	1

The McLaren F1 LM has a large rear wing to help it stick to the road.

The Mercedes-Benz SLR McLaren features swing-wing doors that swing both forward and upward.

Fact >>>>>

In 2000 U.S. sports car manufacturer Saleen introduced the S7. It is considered the first true American supercar.

SUPERCAR DESIGN

What makes a supercar fast? The car's design is one major factor. A supercar might have a very lightweight body and specially designed tires. But the engine design plays the largest role in delivering high speed. Most modern supercars have a V-8 or a V-12 engine. The "V" refers to the position of the *cylinders* to one another. Other engines have a W shape. This shape is usually formed with two V-shaped banks of cylinders placed side by side. The numbers, such as 8 and 12, refer to the number of cylinders in an engine. Generally the more cylinders an engine has, the more *horsepower* it can produce.

Engines are also measured with the letter "L," which stands for liters. This measurement tells you how many liters of air an engine can suck into its cylinders during two full revolutions of its *pistons*.

Most supercar engines use turbochargers or superchargers. A turbocharger can boost the power of an engine without adding a great deal of weight. It does this by pushing more air and fuel into an engine's cylinders. A supercharger basically has the same purpose. The difference is that a supercharger gets its power from a belt connected to the engine. A turbocharger runs by using the exhaust flow of the engine to power a fan.

Fact >>>>>

The horsepower of an average passenger car doesn't come close to the horsepower of a supercar. A 2014 Toyota Camry with a 3.5L V-6 engine produces 268 horsepower.

Supercar Engines

Model	Engine Type	Horsepower	Top Speed	0-62 mph (0-100 kph)
2011 SSC Tuatara	7L V-8	1,350	267 mph (430 kph) (projected)	2.8 seconds
2009 SSC Ultimate Aero TT	6.3L V-8	1,287	267 mph (430 kph)	2.5 seconds
2013 Lamborghini Aventador Mansory Carbonado	6.5L V-12	1,250	236 mph (380 kph)	2.6 seconds
2010 Bugatti Veyron 16.4 Super Sport	8L W-16	1,200	258 mph (415 kph) (*electronically limited to protect tires)	2.2 seconds
2011 Hennessey Venom GT	6.2L V-8	1,200	272 mph (438 kph) (projected)	2.4 seconds

2010 Bugatti Veyron engine

cylinder—a hollow area inside an engine in which fuel burns to create power
horsepower—a unit for measuring an engine's power
piston—part of an engine that moves up and down within a cylinder; a full revolution includes both the up and down movement

9

Chassis

A car's frame is called a chassis. It sits under the body. Most supercar chassis have similar parts. Manufacturers start the chassis design with hollow tubular frames. These frames are then covered with aluminum sheeting that has been honeycombed. Metal that has been through the honeycombing process has hundreds of tiny holes in it. Supercar chassis designed in this way keep the cars' weight low, which means the cars will have more speed. A lightweight body is then formed over the top of the chassis.

Body Design

A supercar's body design also can help increase performance. Manufacturers design the body with *aerodynamics* in mind. They use lightweight materials, such as *carbon fiber*.

Formula 1 race cars have inspired many supercar designs. The Ferrari Enzo has a "shovel-nose" front end that cuts through the air. The Ferrari F40 and F50 have a large rear wing. This wing provides downforce, which pushes down the car's back end. The car can then grip the road better.

Ferrari introduced the Enzo in 2002. Ferrari built 399 Enzos.

aerodynamics—the ability of something to move easily through the air
carbon fiber—a strong, lightweight man-made material

Tires

Most supercars have specially designed custom tires. The Koenigsegg Agera R has a set of specially designed Michelin wheels. The wheels are hollow and made of carbon fiber. Many supercars have extra wide tires. These tires provide better grip and handling because more tire surface is in contact with the road.

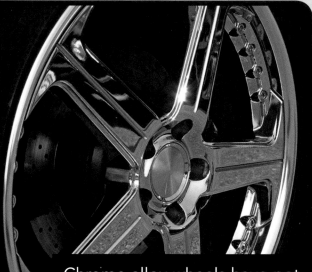

Chrome alloy wheels have not only chrome, but also at least one other metal type.

Interior

Manufacturers usually call the interior of a supercar the cockpit. That's because it is more like a jet's cockpit than the interior of most cars. It is often stripped down to the bare essentials. Sometimes the accelerator and brake pedals are made with holes in them. These small details all help make supercars as light as possible.

Fact >>>>>

When it was introduced in 1987, the Ferrari
F40 was one of the lightest cars in the world.
It weighed 2,425 pounds (1,100 kilograms).
The doors had plastic windows, and its
interior was stripped down to reduce weight.

SPEEDING THROUGH HISTORY

Car manufacturers have used the term "supercar" for decades. Car journalists first used the term to describe a new class of high-performance cars in the mid-1900s. But the term didn't become widely used until the 1960s.

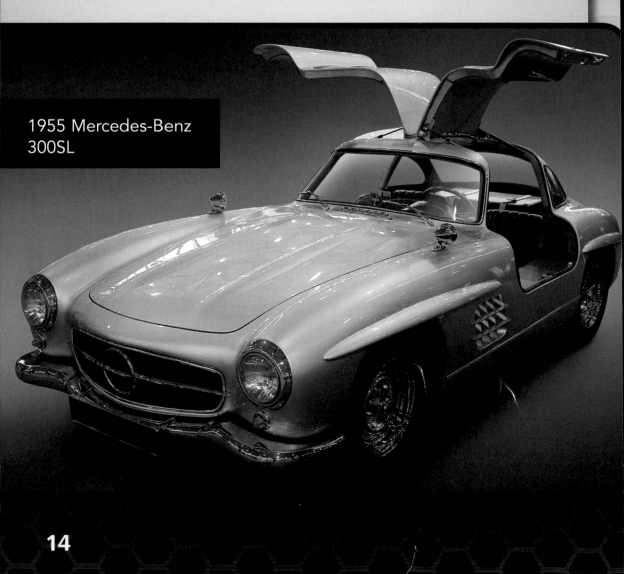

1955 Mercedes-Benz 300SL

Many sports cars from the 1950s were leaders in performance and technology. They were setting a high standard for sports cars. Designers were experimenting with new aerodynamic body shapes and developing more powerful engines. Today many people consider these cars to be classic supercars. The 1954 Mercedes-Benz 300SL Coupe was originally designed as a lightweight race car. The 1958 250 Ferrari Testarossa was available as both a race car and a street car.

In 1965 the Lamborghini Miura changed the world of supercars forever. Company founder Ferruccio Lamborghini developed this futuristic car. Ferruccio was a collector of high-performance cars. While very impressed with these vehicles, Lamborghini believed he could do better. The Miura wowed the crowds at the 1966 Geneva Motor Show with its exciting design. Its most radical design feature was the placement of the engine. The Miura was the first car to have a mid-engine. The car became the fastest *production car* in the world with a top speed of 171 miles (275 km) per hour.

Fact »»»»

The 1966 Lamborghini Miura was one of the first cars to be called a supercar by the writers of *CAR* magazine.

production car—a car that is generally available for the public to buy; a production car is usually built in a factory

Strong-spirited competition between Ferrari and Lamborghini inspired several supercars in the 1970s and 1980s. They included the 1984 Ferrari Testarossa, the 1985 Lamborghini Countach QV17, and the 1984 Ferrari 288 GTO.

1974 Lamborghini Countach LP400

The 1974 Lamborghini Countach LP400 was considered the leading supercar of its time. Its wedgelike body was a completely new design. Two large air ducts were cut out behind the side windows. They allowed air in to help cool the supercar's massive V-12 engine. The engine was mounted backward behind the driver, which helped improve traction. The Countach was the first production car with scissor doors that lifted up toward the front.

Designer Marcello Gandini added these doors not just for style, but also for practical reasons. The car's width would have made standard doors difficult to use in tight parking spaces.

1987 Ferrari F40

The 1987 Ferrari F40 was created to celebrate Ferrari's 40th anniversary. It was the first street-legal car to reach a top speed of more than 200 miles (322 km) per hour. Its long, thin nose and full-width rear wing helped the car grip the road at high speeds. Side air ducts allowed air to flow right through the car, reducing *drag*.

The Lamborghini Countach remained in production until 1990.

drag—the force created when air strikes a moving object; drag slows down moving objects

Power Boost

Car manufacturers began developing more powerful supercars in the 1990s and early 2000s. The use of lightweight materials such as carbon fiber became much more common. Manufacturers also were designing more powerful turbocharged engines. The 1992 Bugatti EB110 had four separate turbochargers on its V-12 engine. By the mid-1990s supercars such as the Dauer 962 LM were reaching speeds near 250 miles (402 km) per hour.

One of the most impressive supercars of its time was the 1993 McLaren F1. With a V-12 engine, it offered race car performance on the streets. On March 31, 1998, an F1 broke the record for the world's fastest production car. It reached a blazing 240.1 miles (386 km) per hour.

Fact >>>>>

The 1993 McLaren F1 had a gold-plated engine bay for heat reflection. This feature protected the engine from overheating at high speeds.

Important Dates in Supercar History

1948   Ferrari introduces its first street-legal car, the 166 Inter.

1965   Lamborghini unveils its 1966 Miura.

1974   Lamborghini introduces the powerful and stylish Countach LP400.

1987   The Ferrari F40 becomes the first street-legal car to reach 200 miles (322 km) per hour.

1998   The McLaren F1 posts a top speed of 240.1 miles (386 km) per hour.

2000   Race car driver Steve Saleen and his team create the S7. It is the first truc American-built supercar.

2010   The Bugatti Veyron Super Sport sets a world speed record for production cars, reaching 267.8 miles (431 km) per hour.

The McLaren F1 was a standout supercar of the 1990s.

MODERN SUPERCARS

Today's supercars push the limits in all areas, including performance, technology, and looks. Car manufacturers race to break speed records set by their competitors. They also try to attract potential customers with unique design features.

2006 Gumpert Apollo

The German-built Gumpert Apollo burst onto the supercar scene in 2006. At the time it was one of the lightest supercars. The car weighs less than 2,600 pounds (1,179 kg). In comparison the 2006 Lamborghini Murciélago LP640 weighs more than 3,500 pounds (1,588 kg). The Gumpert Apollo's *chromoly* frame weighs only 216 pounds (98 kg). The car's *fiberglass* body also helps keep its weight low. The Apollo reaches a blistering top speed of 224 miles (360 km) per hour.

2011 Lamborghini Aventador LP700-4

Lamborghini rolled out the Lamborghini Aventador in 2011. The one-piece driver's cockpit is called a monocoque. The Roadster version has two removable roof panels. With the top down, drivers can hear the roar of the massive V-12 engine. The car's top speed is 217 miles (349 km) per hour. The car's movable spoiler adjusts to three different settings depending on the speed the car is traveling.

The 2006 Gumpert Apollo's wide body gives it a sturdy look.

chromoly—a mixture of two metals called chromium and molybdenum

fiberglass—a strong, lightweight material made from thin threads of glass

2011 Pagani Huayra

Italian carmaker Pagani named its supercar after the ancient Incan god of wind, Huayra-tata. The car's body is designed like a wing. Its forward-positioned cockpit and high front end allow the car to slice through the air like the wing of a jet. A Mercedes-Benz-designed V-12 engine gives it mega power. Its top speed is more than 230 miles (370 km) per hour. The Huayra was named "*Hypercar* of the Year" by the magazine *Top Gear* in 2012.

The 2011 Huayra sits on display at a show in Monaco in 2011.

Fact »»»»

Most supercars have an electronic control that limits their speed. With this control off, many supercars can go 10 to 15 miles (16 to 24 km) per hour faster.

2013 Koenigsegg Agera R

Swedish car manufacturer Koenigsegg entered the upper level of supercars in 2011 with the Koenigsegg Agera R. The car has a top recorded speed of 260 miles (418 km) per hour. But manufacturers believe the car actually could reach 273 miles (440 km) per hour. The car also has impressive acceleration speeds. It can go from 0 to 200 miles (322 km) per hour in 17.68 seconds.

hypercar—a top-end supercar that surpasses other supercars in several categories, such as performance and design

A Need for Speed

The record for the fastest car on the planet usually isn't held long by any car. It seems as soon as one car sets the record, another comes right along and smashes it. But it's safe to say that a street-legal car that holds a speed record is almost always a supercar. Some modern supercars are known for their speed.

Bugatti Veyron Super Sport

Bugatti Veyron Super Sport

With a top speed of 267.8 miles (431 km) per hour, the Bugatti Veyron Super Sport is officially the fastest street-legal car in the world. The car broke this record in 2010. At top speed it would go through an entire tank of gas in 10 minutes! It would also burn out all four of its tires in 15 minutes.

Hennessey Venom GT

According to supercar manufacturer Hennessey, its Venom GT was clocked at a mind-boggling 270.49 miles (435.31 km) per hour in February 2014. Although the speed is not officially recognized by Guinness World Records, the Venom GT could be the fastest car in the world. The Hennessey Venom GT also has a faster acceleration than most supercars. It holds a Guinness World Record for standing-start acceleration. It can go from standing still to 186 miles (299 km) per hour in 13.63 seconds.

Veyron vs. Venom

Bugatti Veyron Super Sport
Top Speed: 267.8 mph (431 kph)
Acceleration: 0-60 mph (97 kph) in 2.5 seconds
Engine: 8L W-16; 1,200 horsepower
Price: $2.4 million

Hennessey Venom GT
Top Speed: 270.49 mph (435.31 kph) *unofficial
Acceleration: 0-60 mph (97 kph) in 2.7 seconds
Engine: 6.2L V-8; 1,200 horsepower
Price: $1.25 million

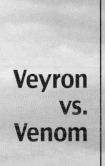

Hennessey Venom GT

The Future of Supercars

Supercar manufacturers are always looking to feature new technology in their cars. Many manufacturers are producing cars that are friendlier to the environment. The use of *biofuels* and other alternatives to gasoline has led to the development of different engines. Electric engines and hybrid engines are becoming more common. Hybrid engines use a mix of electricity and gasoline.

Modern supercars with hybrid engines include the Ferrari LaFerrari, the Porsche 918 Spyder, and the McLaren P1. With these models each manufacturer raced to outdo the others. As they competed, performance, styling, and prices for the cars rose to astonishing levels. Horsepower is just one example. The 2015 P1 produces 903 horsepower, and the 2015 918 Spyder produces 887. And the 2015 LaFerrari? It blasts out 950 horsepower.

The supercar producers at SSC North America plan to chase the world speed record with the SSC Tuatara. The entire body, including the wheels, is made of carbon fiber. The car's manufacturer says the Tuatara can go from 0 to 60 miles (97 km) per hour in 2.5 seconds. They also claim the Tuatara can reach a top speed of 276 miles (444 km) per hour. If it does, it will shatter the record currently held by the Bugatti Veyron Super Sport.

Modern Supercar Price Tags

2005 Maybach Exelero—$8 million

2009 Zenvo ST1—$5.5 million

2013 Lamborghini Veneno—$5.3 million

2010 Koenigsegg CCXR Trevita—$4.85 million

2013 Pagani Zonda Revolucion—$4.5 million

Onlookers in the United Kingdom gather around a McLaren P1 on tour to promote the 2014 movie *Need for Speed*.

biofuel—a fuel made of or produced from plant material

Concept Cars for the Future

The future seems unlimited for supercars. Engineers and designers find inspiration in race cars and even aircraft. They often begin by designing a concept car. These are one-of-a-kind vehicles with cutting-edge technology and design.

Super Auto Shows

Auto shows give manufacturers a chance to show off their concept cars and new models. If the concept cars become popular with car buyers, they may go into production. The North American International Auto Show is held in Detroit, Michigan, every January. It is one of the largest car shows in the United States. There is a section reserved just for supercars.

Most countries in Europe have their own auto shows. They include the Paris Motor Show in France and the Frankfurt Motor Show in Germany. The International Geneva Motor Show held in Geneva, Switzerland, is unique for its wide range of supercars. The Koenigsegg Agera R, Lamborghini Aventador LP700-4, Lamborghini Huracán LP610-4, and the McLaren P1 have all been introduced there.

Each year fans anxiously await the next supercar concepts. With competition so fierce, it's anybody's guess which manufacturer will have the next big hit.

In 2010 Mercedes-Benz unveiled its BIOME concept car at the Los Angeles Auto Show. The material for its body was made from plants grown from specially designed seeds. The material was called Bio-Fibre.

The Lamborghini Aventador LP700 is unveiled at the 2011 International Geneva Motor Show.

GLOSSARY

aerodynamics (air-oh-dy-NA-miks)—the ability of something to move easily through the air

biofuel (BYE-oh-fyoo-uhl)—a fuel made of or produced from plant material

carbon fiber (KAHR-buhn FY-buhr)—a strong, lightweight man-made material

chromoly (KROH-muh-lee)—a mixture of two metals called chromium and molybdenum

cylinder (SI-luhn-duhr)—a hollow area inside an engine in which fuel burns to create power

drag (DRAG)—the force created when air strikes a moving object; drag slows down moving objects

fiberglass (FY-buhr-glas)—a strong, lightweight material made from thin threads of glass

gull-wing doors (GUHL-WING DORZ)—car doors hinged at the roof that look like spread bird wings when opened

horsepower (HORSS-pou-ur)—a unit for measuring an engine's power

hypercar (HYE-pur-kar)—a top-end supercar that surpasses other supercars in several categories, such as performance or design

piston (PIS-tuhn)—the part of an engine that moves up and down within a cylinder

production car (pruh-DUHK-shuhn KAR)—a car that is generally available for the public to buy; a production car is usually built in a factory

spoiler (SPOY-lur)—a wing-shaped part attached to the front or rear of a sports car that improves the car's handling and keeps air from lifting the car off the road

sports car (SPORTS KAR)—a street-legal car that is designed for high-performance

READ MORE

Graham, Ian. *Cars*. Design and Engineering for STEM. Chicago, Ill.: Capstone Heinemann Library, 2013.

Kenney, Karen Latchana. *The Science of Car Racing*. The Science of Speed. North Mankato, Minn.: Capstone Press, 2014.

Savery, Annabel. *Supercars*. It's Amazing! Mankato, Minn.: Smart Apple Media, 2013.

INTERNET SITES

FactHound offers a safe, fun way to find Internet sites related to this book. All of the sites on FactHound have been researched by our staff.

Here's all you do:

Visit *www.facthound.com*

Type in this code: 9781491420140

 Check out projects, games and lots more at **www.capstonekids.com**

INDEX